SUMMER BLAST

Getting Ready for Kindergarten

Author
Jodene Smith, M.A.

SHELL EDUCATION

Publishing Credits

Corinne Burton, M.A.Ed., *President*; Emily R. Smith, M.A.Ed., *Content Director*; Jennifer Wilson, *Senior Editor*; Robin Erickson, *Multimedia Designer*; Valerie Morales; *Assistant Editor*; Stephanie Bernard, *Assistant Editor*; Amber Goff, *Editorial Assistant*; Mindy Duits, *Cover Concept*

Image Credits

All images from iStock and Shutterstock

Shell Education
A division of Teacher Created Materials
5482 Argosy Avenue
Huntington Beach, CA 92649
www.tcmpub.com/shell-education
ISBN 978-1-4258-1550-9

updated 2026
Printed by: 590835
Printed in: China

Table of Contents

Welcome to

SUMMER BLAST

Getting Ready for Kindergarten

Summer Blast was designed to help your child prepare for the year ahead.

How to Use This Book

- Review the Parent and Family Pages (pages 4–12) for fun ways to learn and explore as a family. Every family outing, visit to a park, or car ride provides opportunities for your child (and you!) to play games, learn more about the world around you, and have fun as a family.
- There are nine weeks of activities to keep your child learning over the summer. At the start of each week, review the weekly overview. It summarizes the skills your child will practice throughout the week and will help you be prepared to support their efforts.
- Each week includes nine activity pages that cover letters, reading, writing, and numbers. Also included are a weekly game and game cards for your child to play with friends and family.

Summer Learning Made Fun

Here are some of the topics covered in this book to help prepare your child for kindergarten:

Language Arts/Reading

- Begin sounding out simple words.
- Identify and say rhyming words.
- Recognize and name some upper- and lowercase letters.
- Follow reading from left to right and turn pages in order.
- Use illustrations to retell stories, including important details (characters, setting, problem and solution).
- Ask and answer questions about important details in a story.
- Participate in conversations, offering opinions, ideas, and feelings.

Math

- Name and write numbers 1–20.
- Count to 20.
- Identify 2D shapes.

Supporting Your Child

Keep these tips in mind as you work with your child this summer.

General Tips

- Set aside a specific time each day to work on the activities.
- Have your child complete one or two pages at a time, rather than an entire week's worth of activity pages.
- Keep all practice sessions positive. Encourage your child to do their best work and compliment the effort that goes into learning.
- Help your child with instructions, if necessary. If your child is having difficulty understanding what to do, work through some of the problems together.
- Encourage your child's creativity! Create opportunities for your child to act out stories they read, draw pictures of concepts they learn, and use their imagination to learn about the world around them.

Math Tips

How You Can Help	What You Can Say
Provide manipulatives (beans, cereal, pennies) for your child to count.	How many beans are there?
Have your child write a number to match the number of items they counted.	You counted 9 beans. How do you write the number nine?
Provide opportunities for your child to count backward from a given number.	Count back from 10. When counting back, what number comes next?

Language Arts and Reading Tips

How You Can Help	What You Can Say
Encourage your child to find a given letter throughout a book they are reading.	Can you find the letter D on this page?
Help your child recognize rhyming words. Say a word and ask them to name a word that rhymes.	What is a word that rhymes with *cat*?
Help your child recognize the beginning sound in a word. Then ask them to name other words with that beginning sound.	What is the first sound in the word *dog*? What other words start with the sound /d/?

Enjoy the time learning with your child this summer. Kindergarten will be here before you know it!

Things to Do as a Family

General Skills

- Make sure your child gets plenty of sleep. Children this age need between 10 and 13 hours of sleep each night. Even in the summer, establish a nightly bedtime routine that involves relaxing activities such as a warm shower or bath or reading a story.
- Help your child become organized and responsible by setting a good example for them. Have places to keep important things. Make to-do lists of your chores or errands. When your child sees you taking the time to organize and set aside time for these things, they will recognize that organization and responsibility are important to practice.

Reading Skills

- Create an alphabet book with your child. Go through old magazines, newspapers, advertisements, etc. to find an image for each letter of the alphabet. Help your child cut out the images and glue them into an alphabet book of their very own.
- Set a reading time for the entire family at least every other day. Have your child read familiar words or letters. Point to words that they may already know (or words that are similar to ones they already know) and have them sound them out.

Mathematics Skills

- Help your child practice counting, whenever possible. You can do this in everyday situations like counting the number of stairs or steps, counting how many silverware pieces are at the dinner table, etc.
- Involve your child in grocery shopping. Ask them to help solve basic mathematical problems. For example, "I have two apples in my hands. You have two apples in yours. How many apples do we have altogether?"

Writing Skills

- Since children this age are just learning to write, introduce writing as a fun activity instead of a boring task or assignment. Have your child practice learning the shapes of letters through sensory activities. For example, you could pour an impressionable substance (this could be salt, flour, sugar, pudding, shaving cream, etc.) into a cookie tray and let kids get their hands messy while learning to write individual letters.
- Supply your child with writing tools that better fit their hands to help develop their fine motor skills. Normal-length pencils are often too large and are awkward for smaller hands to hold. Golf pencils, broken crayons, and small markers work especially well and will make writing more comfortable.

Family Outings

A Trip to a Zoo

Before your trip, create a Zoo Bingo card. Include pictures of a variety of animals you will see at the zoo. Bring the Zoo Bingo card with you. Have your child pick out a set of stickers from the zoo gift shop to use as markers for the bingo card. As you spend the day exploring, have your child place a sticker on each animal you come across. When they get bingo, celebrate the accomplishment!

A Trip to a Museum

Play a family game in an area or room of the museum. Have your child pick out an artifact or piece of art without telling the other players what it is. The other players then try to guess what the secret item is. Ask for clues that require a yes or no answer. For example, "Does the item have sharp teeth?," or "Is the item made out of clay?" The person who guesses the secret item correctly gets to choose the item in the next room.

A Trip to a Library

Have your child pick out books they have never read (or that you have never read to them). Look over the covers of the books together, paying close attention to the cover art. Ask your child what they think the stories are going to be about based on the covers alone. Then, read the books aloud to your child and see if their guess was correct. Record the books on the Summer Reading Log (pages 10–11).

A Trip to the Park

Before your trip, create a Park Scavenger Hunt. Include a list of items to see and do when you get to the park. For example, "Touch a tree" or "Spot an animal." Bring along a marker and try to check off every item on the list!

A Trip to a Monument or Memorial

If you're able to visit a monument or memorial with your child, be sure to make it come alive for them. Ahead of time, look up some interesting stories about the person who is honored by the monument/memorial. Focus on stories about the person's childhood or early accomplishments, as those will be more relatable to your child. As you stand and look at the monument/memorial, tell the stories and ask your child to describe what kind of monument/memorial they think could be built for them someday!

Family-Friendly Apps

Apps

Epic

Kids can explore the world's largest digital library through this fun, kid-safe, interactive reading app!

Lingokids

Kids can explore over 3,000 interactive games covering 650+ learning objectives including math, literacy, science, engineering, art, music, and more!

Kids Puzzles Games Puzzingo

These puzzles focus on improving vocabulary, cognitive skills, spatial recognition, and matching.

and Websites

Websites

ABCya

http://www.abcya.com

This site focuses on a variety of reading and mathematical skills through fun games, puzzles, mazes, and exercises.

Funbrain

http://www.funbrain.com/games

Fun, arcade-style games covering a variety of concepts at all grade levels make this a great website for busy families.

Games to Play on the Go

Hunt for the Alphabet

Have your child help you find all the letters of the alphabet. Look for each letter in order on billboards, license plates, store signs, etc. This will encourage letter recognition as well as learning and understanding alphabetical order. This game can also be played with numbers.

I Spy (with a Twist)

This is a favorite on-the-go game. However, it can get boring when you play with just colors, so add a small twist. Instead of always spying a colored object, spy objects that are certain shapes, distances, or textures. You might say, "I spy an oval." Or, "I spy something that begins with the letter b." Or even, "I spy something bumpy." It certainly makes the game more interesting. And don't forget to allow yes/no critical-thinking questions. For example, "Is the object high in the sky?" Or, "Is the object inside the car?"

Who Am I?

Think of a person your child knows. This can be a friend, neighbor, grandparent, or even a fictional or historical character they love. Then, give your child clues about that person using hair color, gender, whether they wears glasses, etc. Keep giving clues until your child guesses who the person is.

Animal Sounds

Make an animal sound and have your child guess the animal. You can make the game a bit more interesting by adding points. For example, you could reward 2 points if they correctly name the animal within 3 guesses and 5 points if they correctly name it on the first guess.

Would You Rather

Have your child choose between two scenarios, such as "Would you rather have wings or a tail?" or "Would you rather have a pet dolphin or tiger?" To encourage critical thinking, have your child explain why they choose or did not choose each scenario.

Summer Reading Log

Keep track of summer reading. If you fill the pages, start a new reading log on your own!

Date	Title	Number of Pages

Summer Reading Log

Keep track of summer reading. If you fill the pages, start a new reading log on your own!

Date	Title	Number of Pages

Books to Read Aloud

If you love learning about handling worries and big emotions, try

Wemberly Worried
by Kevin Henkes.

Everyone worries! In this story, Wemberly, a little mouse, has a lot of worries! This story helps young children learn how to find comfort and to better understand their big emotions.

If you love learning about silly monsters that do naughty things, try

Don't Push the Button
by Bill Cotter.

This fun, interactive book stars Larry the purple monster. There is only one rule for Larry—don't push the button. Children will love the hands-on experience this story provides as Larry asks them to help him push the button when no one is looking. The silly consequences of pushing the button are sure to keep your child giggling.

If you love learning about imaginative places, try

Where the Wild Things Are
by Maurice Sendak.

Explore the power of imagination in this story of a little boy named Max and his adventure to the land of the Wild Things. Winner of the Caldecott Medal, the beautiful and detailed illustrations make Max's imagination come to life as he sets sail on a wild adventure and explores a new land.

If you love learning about silly animals, try

Don't Let the Pigeon Drive the Bus!
by Mo Willems.

This book will have your child (and you) laughing out loud, as a very determined pigeon tries to convince the reader to let him drive the bus. The simple but clever illustrations make each of the pigeon's emotions come to life as he continues to try and persuade the reader. Have your child participate in the story by having them say "no" out loud to each of the pigeon's requests. Your child will laugh aloud at the pigeon's reactions to the constant "no" response to his many arguments for being able to drive the bus.

If you love counting, try

The Very Hungry Caterpillar
by Eric Carle.

A hungry little caterpillar eats his way through plenty of fruit and various snacks like cheese, lollipops, and salami. This book is not only visually stimulating for children, but also helps introduce counting in an enjoyable way.

Week 1

This week, you will practice these important skills:

- writing the letters *A* and *B*
- reading a story
- drawing a picture of favorite things
- making dot art
- matching colors to numbers
- counting to ten
- naming shapes
- connecting the dots
- playing rhyme games

Practice A and B

Directions: Trace and write the letters. Color the *Aa*'s red. Color the *Bb*'s blue.

A a A a

B b B b

A a

b b

a B c

B A

X Marks the Spot

Directions: Listen to an adult read the story. Then, talk about the questions.

"Argh!" yells Captain Max. "Where is my treasure box?"

"Try the map," says Polly. "X marks the spot!"

Just then, the wind blows. The *X* on the map is gone.

"The *X* isn't a treasure. It's a crumb!" says Polly.

"Argh!" cries Max.

1. Who is in the story?
2. Where does the story happen?
3. What happens in the story?

Favorite Treat

Directions: Draw a treat. Trace the word. Share your drawing.

treat

Talk About It!

What did you draw? Why did you draw that? What details can you add?

Dot Art

Materials

- white paper
- paint
- a cotton swab (or a pencil with an eraser tip)

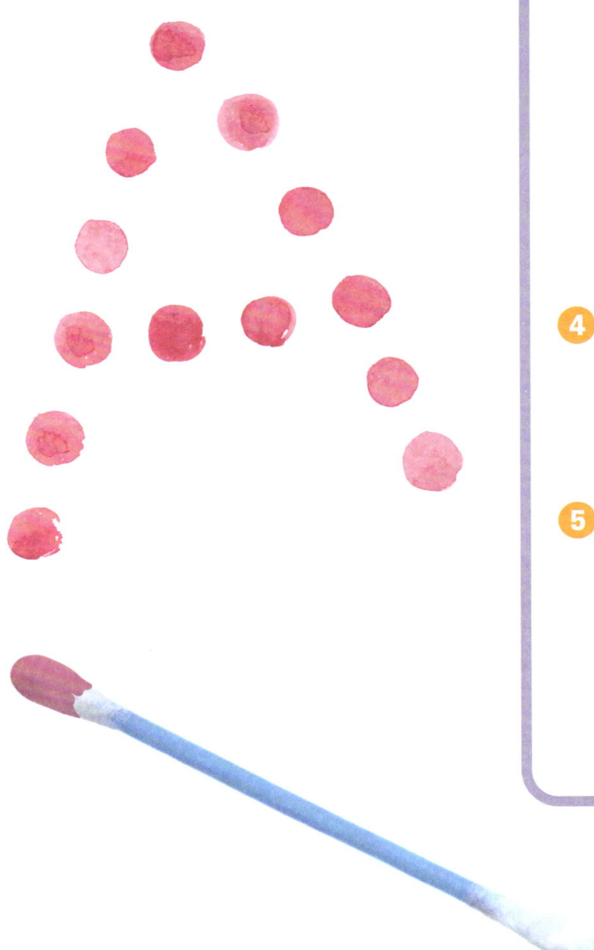

Directions

1. Write the letter your name begins with on a sheet of paper. Write it as large as possible.
2. Talk about words that begin with the letter.
3. Dip a cotton swab in the paint. Tap the cotton swab along the lines of the letter to form dots. Make dots on all the lines of the letter.
4. Allow the paint to dry. Then, share your art with a friend.
5. You may wish to repeat these steps for other letters in the alphabet.

House Number Match

Directions: Color the picture.

Color Code

1 = red
2 = yellow
3 = blue
4 = green
5 = brown
6 = black

Crazy Counting

Directions: Count.

1. Count to 10 in a "baby" voice.

2. Count to 10 in a "scary" voice.

3. Count to 10 in a "silly" voice.

4. Point to the numbers as you count.

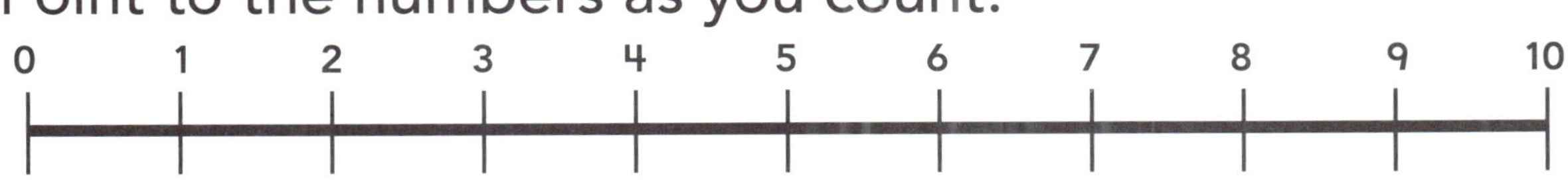

Shapes Everywhere!

Directions: Touch each shape. Say its name.

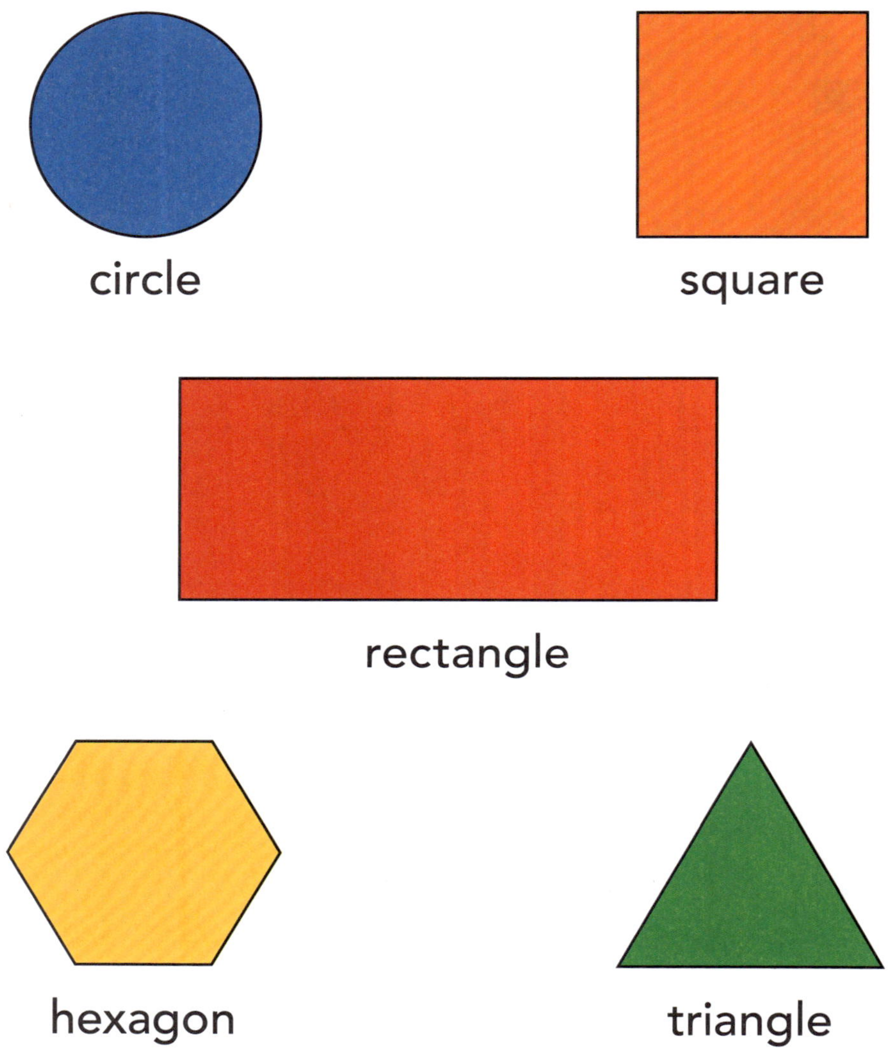

Talk About It!

What sound does each shape's name start with?

Find the Picture

Directions: Sing the ABC song. Connect the dots. Color the picture.

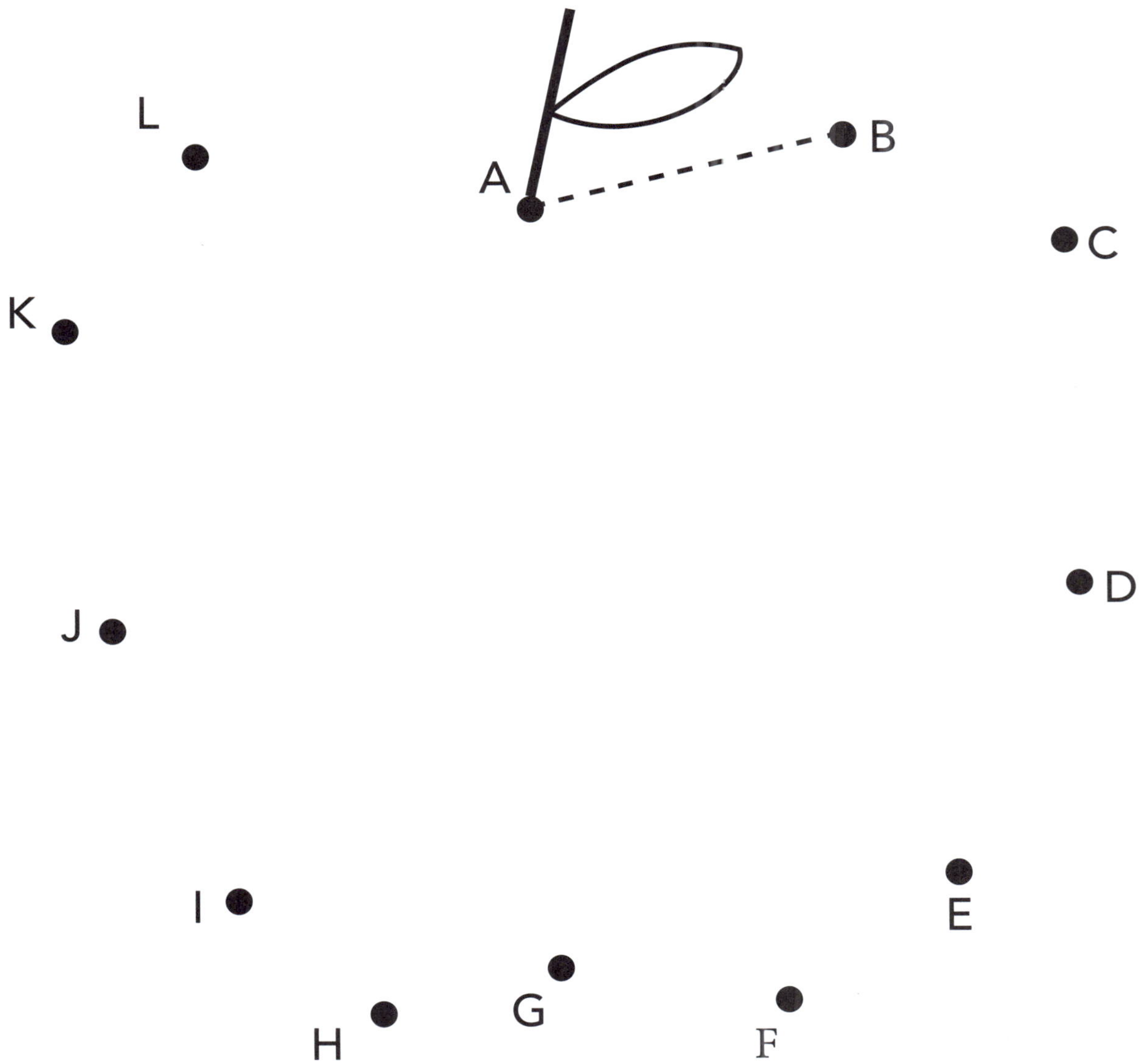

Talk About It!

What different colors do apples come in?

Go Rhyme

Number of Players

2

Materials

- *Picture Cards Set 1* (page 103)
- *Picture Cards Set 2* (page 105)

Directions

1. Cut apart the Picture Cards Set 1 on page 103 or Picture Cards Set 2 on page 105. Shuffle and distribute them evenly to each player. **Note:** If you choose to play with more than two people, use both sets of cards.
2. Lay down any pairs of rhymes from the cards in your hand.
3. Take turns asking one another for words that rhyme with cards left in your hand.

   "Do you have a card that rhymes with *fan*?"
4. If the other player has a card that rhymes, then the card must be given to the person asking.
5. Continue to play until all the rhyme pairs have been matched.
6. Challenge each other to think of another word that rhymes with each pair to make the game more difficult.

Week 2

This week, you will practice these important skills:

- writing the letters *C* and *D*
- reading a nonfiction text
- illustrating things you enjoy
- observing plants
- reading numbers in order
- counting items
- tracing shapes
- identifying and drawing things that are blue
- playing an action game

Practice C and D

Directions: Trace and write the letters. Then, match the letters.

C c C c

D d D d

C	d
D	c
D	c
C	d

The Best Invention

Directions: Listen to an adult read the story. Then, talk about the questions.

The bicycle is the best invention. There are bikes for all ages. Babies can even ride in a trailer pulled by a bike. You can pedal with your feet. Some bikes let you pedal with your hands. Some people may think cars are a better invention. But bikes do not need gas. And you get exercise, too!

1. What are two good things about bikes?
2. Why does the author think bikes are better than cars?
3. If you could invent a new bike, what would it be able to do?

Playtime

Directions: Draw a toy. Trace the word. Share your drawing.

play

Talk About It! What did you draw? Why did you draw that? What details can you add?

Plant Creations

Materials

- clay or molding dough

Directions

1. Color the plant parts below.
2. Go outside and look at a plant. Name the parts of the plant with an adult.
3. Use clay or molding dough to recreate the parts of the plant. Be sure to include a stem, leaves, and a flower.
4. Share your creation with a friend.

stem leaves flower

Number Maze

Directions: Follow the numbers in order.

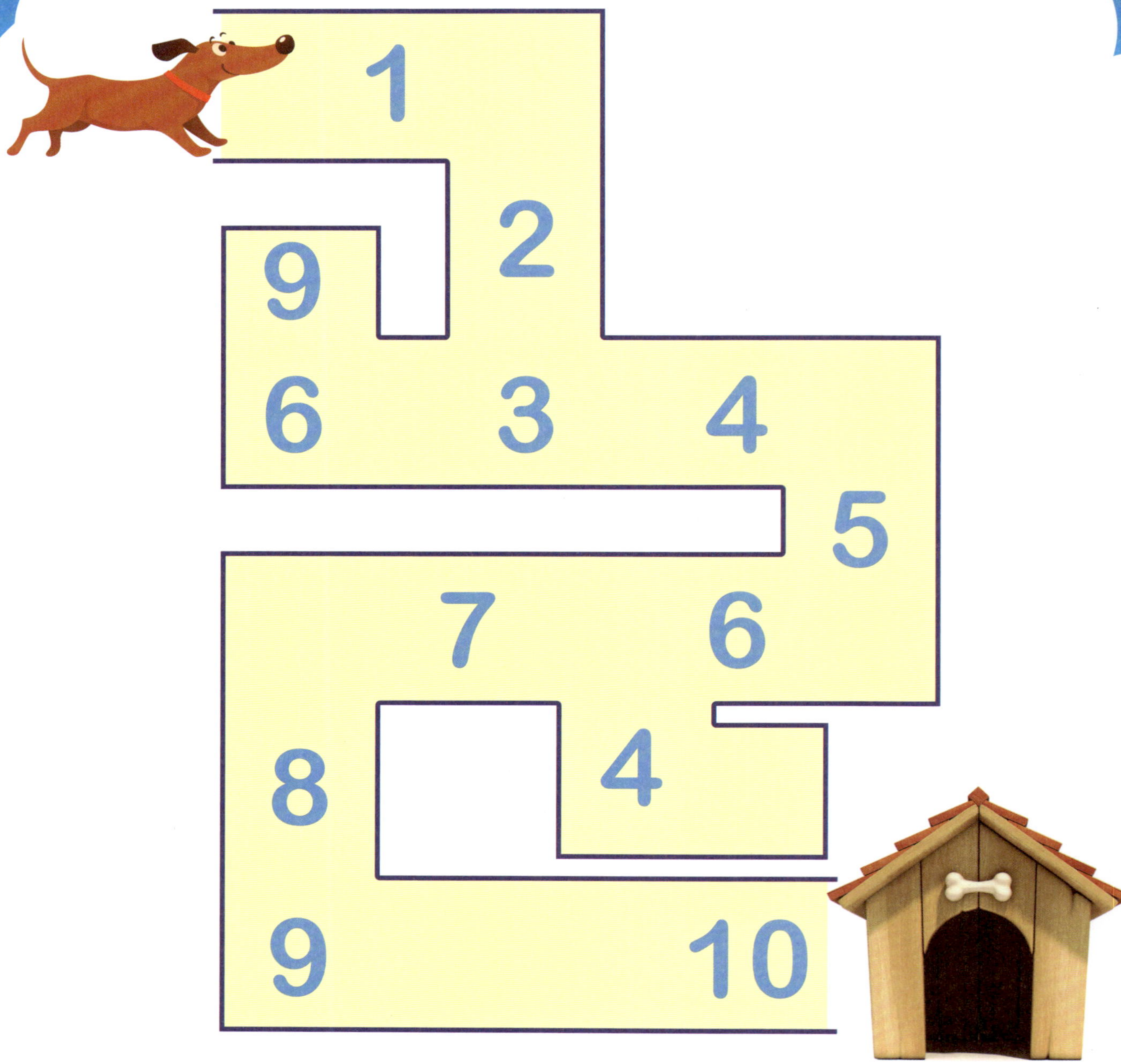

Talk About It! How did you know where to go?

Count and Write

Directions: Count the items. Write the numbers.

Number Bank

1 2 3 4 5

1 

2 

3 

4 

5 

Trace the Shapes

Directions: Trace each shape. Say its name.

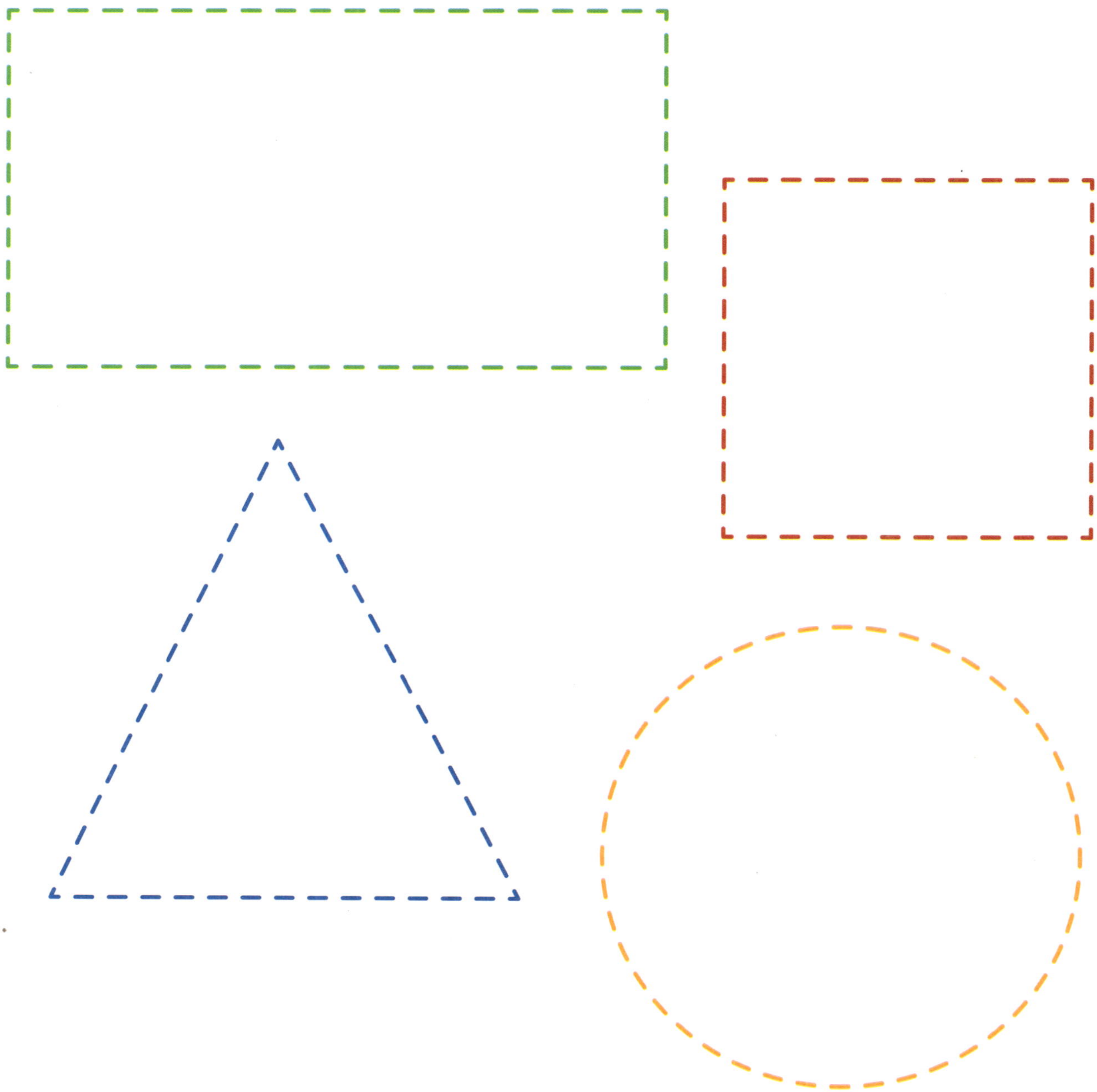

Talk About It! Which shape was your favorite to trace? Why?

Blue, Blue, I See You

Directions: Name things that are blue. Draw them.

Talk About It!

What sound does each thing begin with?

Action Numbers

Number of Players

2–6

Materials

- *Number Cards* (page 107)

Directions

1. Cut apart the *Number Cards* on page 107. (**Note:** Save the cards so that they can be used again with *The Number Game* activity on page 52.) Shuffle the cards and place them facedown in a pile.
2. One player chooses an action from the Action Chart and picks a number card. All players perform the action the specified number of times.
3. Continue turning over the cards and performing actions until all the cards have been used.

Action Chart	
touch toes	stomp feet
jump	turn around
clap	roll over
pat head	walk on toes

Adaptations

- Count out loud together to make the activity easier.
- To make the activity more challenging, have one player turn over a number card and choose an action in secret and then perform the actions. The other players have to count as the player performs the required actions.

Week 3

This week, you will practice these important skills:

- writing the letters *E* and *F*
- reading a story
- illustrating today's weather
- making mirror art
- finding numbers in order
- counting groups of objects
- matching shapes
- coloring objects
- playing a gathering game

Practice E and F

Directions: Trace and write the letters. Color the *Ee*'s red. Color the *Ff*'s blue.

E e E e

F f F f

e f

f E

E F e

g F

Jack and Jill

Directions: Listen to an adult read the poem. Then, answer the questions.

Jack and Jill went up the hill to
fetch a pail of water.

Jack fell down and broke his crown.

And Jill came tumbling after.

1. Are Jack and Jill friends?

   yes no

2. Does Jill fall down first?

   yes no

3. Do Jack and Jill get a pail of water?

   yes no

Weather

Directions: Draw the weather today. Trace the word. Share your drawing.

weather

Talk About It!

What did you draw? Why did you draw that? What details can you add?

It's the Same

Materials

- ruler
- white paper
- paint

Directions

1. Fold a sheet of white paper in the middle. Unfold and smooth flat.
2. Place two small amounts of paint on the right side of the paper. You can use the same color or two different colors.

3. Fold the paper in half again and press down on the paper with your hand.
4. Unfold the paper and allow the paint to dry.
5. Talk about how the paint on both sides of the paper is the same.

Zigzag Parking Lot

Directions: Trace the lines in order.

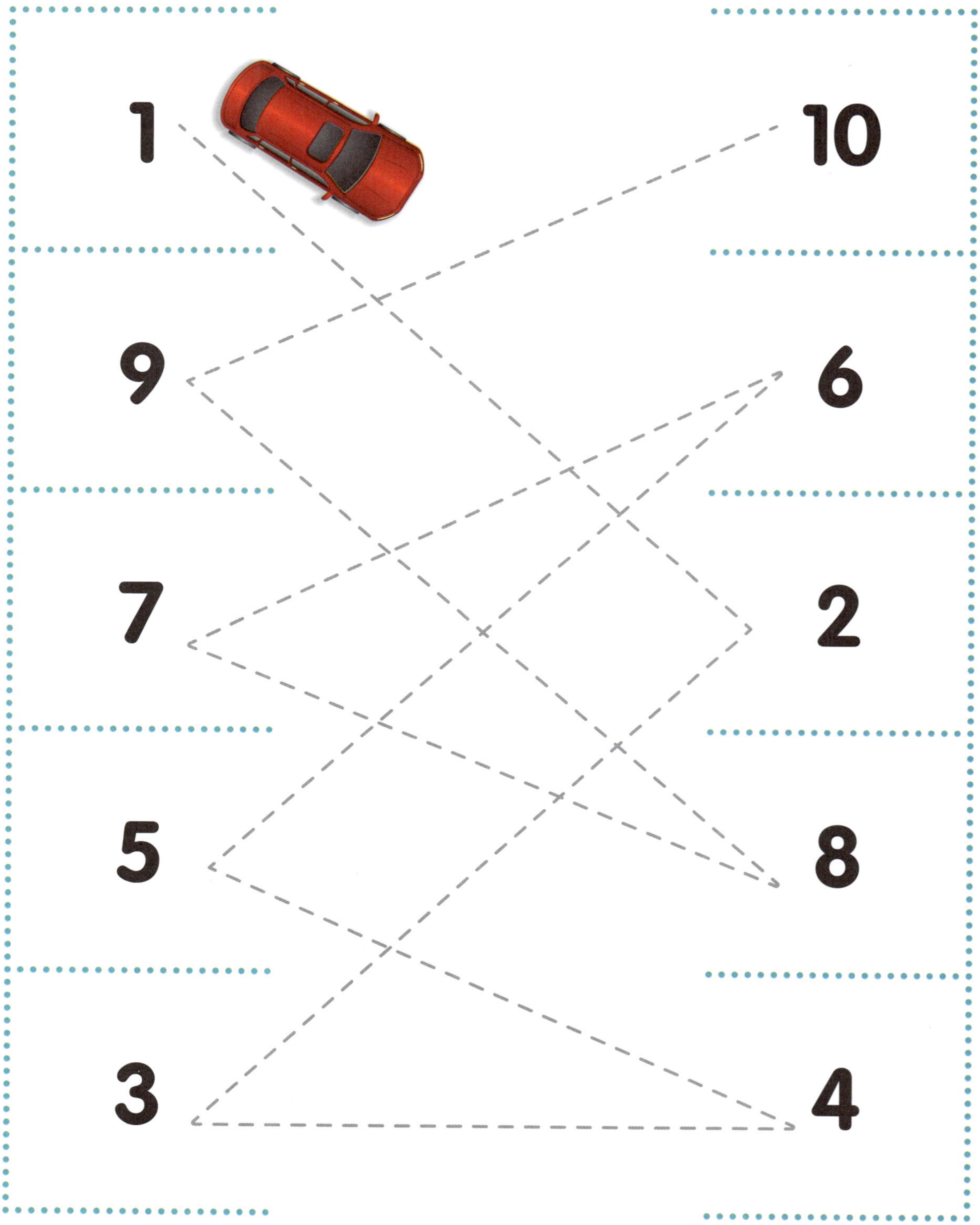

How Many Apples?

Directions: Touch and count the apples. Circle the correct number.

1. 

   6 7 8

2. 

   4 5 6

3. 

   1 2 3

4. 

   4 5 6

Talk About It! How do you like to eat apples? Who do you like to eat them with?

Name the Shapes

Directions: Draw lines to match.

1 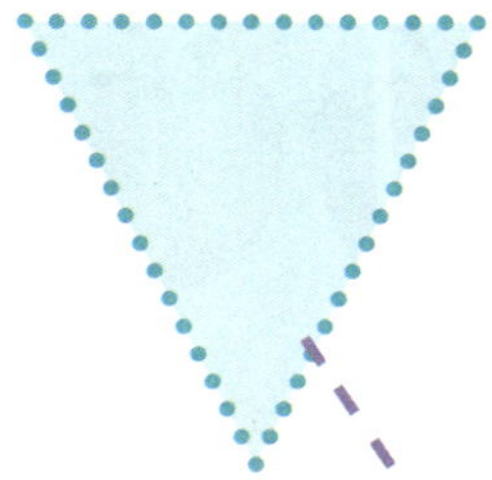

2 

3 

4 

square

rectangle

circle

triangle

Color by Shape

Directions: Color the picture.

● green ■ yellow ▲ brown ◆ blue

The Gathering Game

Number of Players

2–6

Materials

- *Uppercase Letter Cards* (page 109)
- timer
- a bag for each player
- household items

Directions

1. Cut apart the *Uppercase Letter Cards* on page 109. Shuffle the cards and place them facedown in a pile.
2. Provide each player with a bag. Then, set a timer for two minutes.
3. Choose a card. Name the letter on the card and make its sound.
4. Each player goes around the house and gathers as many items that can fit inside the bag that begin with the target sound.
5. Lay out all the items when the timer goes off. Each player names the items gathered. Award one point for each item that matches the target sound.
6. Repeat the game with a different letter card.

Adaptations

- Brainstorm items before setting the timer to make the game easier.
- Look for items around the house that end with the target sound to make it more difficult.

Week 4

This week, you will practice these important skills:

- writing the letters *G* and *H*
- reading a story
- illustrating a friend
- making a blow art painting
- matching numbers to colors
- counting objects
- comparing shapes
- using clues to match items
- playing a numbers game

Practice G and H

Directions: Trace and write the letters. Match the letters.

G g G g

H h H h

G h

H g

H g

G h

The Campout

Directions: Listen to an adult read the story. Then, talk about the questions.

Dad was snoring next to me. But I could not sleep. It was cold in the tent. I was thinking about home. I missed my mom. What if a bear jumped in the tent? How could I wake my dad if a snake slid under my pillow?

I thought morning would never come. But finally, the sun came out. My dad woke up. I told him how scared I was. "Why did you worry?" he asked. "We are just camping in the backyard!"

1. Who are the characters in the story?
2. Why couldn't the boy sleep?
3. Where were the characters?

Friends

Directions: Draw a friend. Trace the word. Share your drawing.

friend

Talk About It!

Who did you draw? Why did you draw them?

Blow Art

Materials

- newspaper
- white paper
- paint
- a straw

Directions

1. Place newspaper down on a hard surface. Then, place a sheet of white paper on top of the newspaper.
2. Place two small amounts of paint on the paper. You can use the same color or two different colors.
3. Place one end of the straw close to the paint but not touching it. Blow into the other end of the straw. Watch the paint spread out as you blow.
4. Experiment blowing lighter and harder. Talk about what happens to the paint as you blow lightly and harder.

Flower Number Match

Directions: Color the picture.

Color Code

1 = green
2 = pink
3 = red
4 = purple
5 = yellow
6 = orange

Sort and Count!

Directions: Touch and count the objects. Circle the correct number.

1. Count the balls. How many?

   2 3 4

2. Count the bats. How many?

   2 3 4

3. Count the suns. How many?

   5 6 7

4. Count the clouds. How many?

   4 5 6

Which Shape?

Directions: Draw a shape in each space.

Three Sides

Four Corners

Curved

Story Time Logic

Directions: Listen to an adult read the clues. Draw a line to match each bear to its owner.

Clues

Maya's bear is not the biggest or smallest.

Sam's bear is the smallest.

1 

Maya

2 

Jane

3 

Sam

The Number Game

Number of Players

2

Materials

- *0–9 Number Cards* (page 107)
- *Calculator Cards* (page 111)
- small markers

Directions

1. Gather the *Number Cards* used with the *Action Numbers* activity on page 32. Save the cards to use for the activity on page 62. Shuffle and place them facedown in a pile.
2. Cut apart the *Calculator Cards* on page 111. All players should have their own cards.
3. One player picks the top card, names the number on the card, and puts a marker on the matching number on their calculator.
4. Take turns until one player has marked all the numbers on their calculator. **Note:** You will need to reshuffle the cards multiple times.

Adaptations

- Play using only numbers 0–5 to make the game easier. Use only 0–5 cards and draw two cards each round.
- To make the game more difficult, add the two numbers together. If the sum is greater than 9, the player loses a turn.

Week 5

This week, you will practice these important skills:

- writing the letters *I* and *J*
- reading a nonfiction text
- illustrating a book character
- tracing shapes
- matching colors to numbers
- filling jars with dots
- creating shapes
- sorting objects
- playing a counting game

Practice I and J

Directions: Trace and write the letters. Color the *Ii*'s red. Color the *Jj*'s blue.

I i I i

J j J j

I j

j i

I i J

J k

Good Hunters

Directions: Listen to an adult read the story. Then, talk about the questions.

Tigers are big, wild cats. Most tigers have orange, black, and white stripes.

Tigers are good hunters. They have large claws. And their teeth are sharp. They can hunt in the dark. They hunt for monkeys, fish, and deer.

1. What are tigers?
2. What color stripes can tigers have?
3. What do tigers hunt for?

Book Time

Directions: Draw a book character. Trace the word. Share your drawing.

book

Talk About It!

Which character did you draw? Why did you draw that character?

Hidden Shape

Materials

- white paper
- white crayon
- watercolor paints
- household items of various shapes (for example, a lid)

Directions

1. Find an object that has a shape you know. For example, a lid is in the shape of a circle.
2. Lay the object on the paper.
3. Trace around the object with a white crayon. **Note:** You will not be able to see the drawing.
4. Paint the entire paper with watercolor paint in any color. See the shape appear! You may wish to repeat this activity with multiple objects.

Number Search

Directions: Use different colors to draw circles around the numbers.

Color Code

1 = red	3 = green
2 = blue	4 = yellow

1 2 3

3 4 1

2 3 4 1

2 4

Fill a Jar

Directions: Draw dots to fill the jar.

1. Fill the jar with 6 dots.

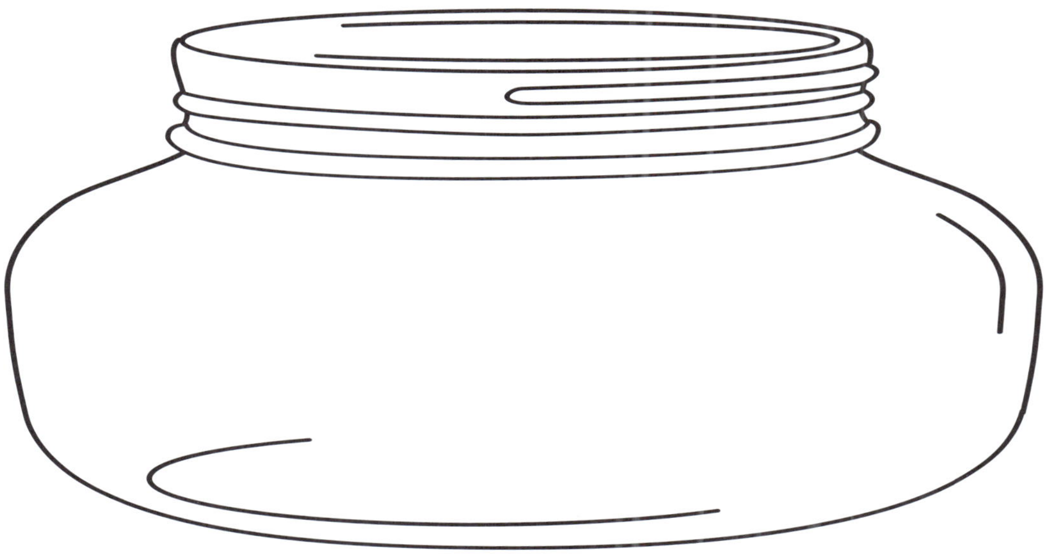

2. Fill the jar with 9 dots.

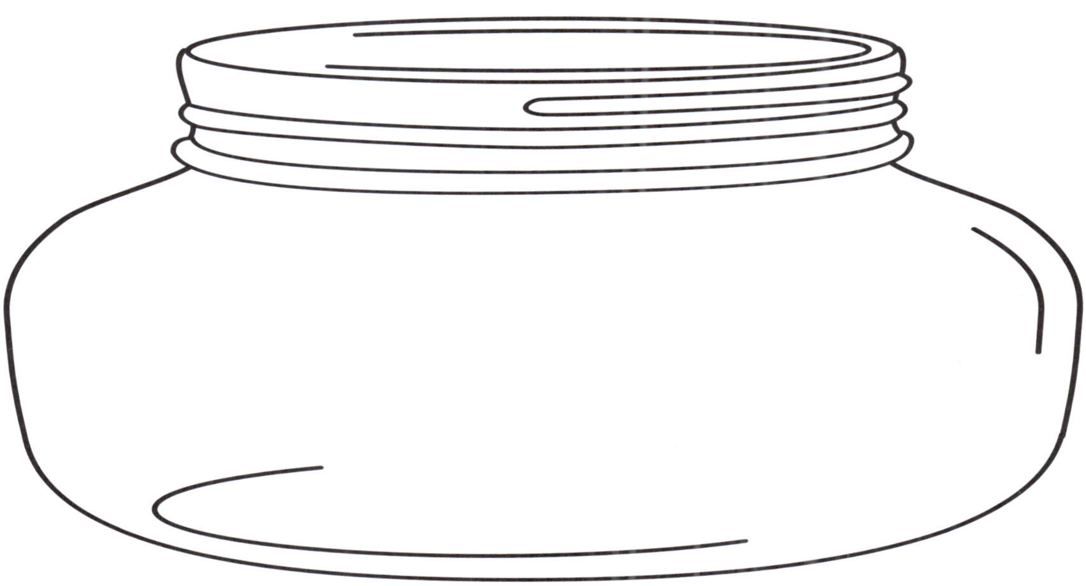

Make the Shapes

Directions: Draw the shapes.

1. Draw a square in the middle of the box.
2. Draw a circle inside the square.
3. Draw a rectangle above the square.
4. Draw a triangle on each side of the square.

square rectangle triangle circle

Does Not Belong

Directions: Make an X on the pictures that do not belong.

1. Which is not a fruit?

2. Which is not an insect?

3. Which is not a house?

4. Which is not a cat?

Fill Your Basket

Number of Players

2

Materials

- *Number Cards* (previously used)
- *Basket Cards* (page 113)
- small counters such as O-shaped cereal or paper clips

Directions

1. Gather the *Number Cards* used from the *Action Number* game on page 32 and *The Numbers Game* on page 52. Shuffle them and place them facedown in a pile.
2. Cut apart the *Basket Cards* on page 113 and give one to each player.
3. The youngest player goes first. Choose a card and place that many counters in your basket.
4. Take turns choosing cards and placing counters in the basket until one player has reached 20 counters. **Note:** You may need to reshuffle the cards during the game.

Adaptations

- Play to a lower number such as 10 to make the game easier.
- Count how many more are needed to get to 20 after each turn to make the game more difficult.

Week 6

This week, you will practice these important skills:

- writing the letters *L* and *M*
- reading a poem
- illustrating something that makes you happy
- tracing the letter *W*
- matching colors to numbers
- counting objects
- coloring different shapes
- connecting the dots
- playing I Spy games

Practice L and M

Directions: Trace and write the letters. Match.

L l L l

M m M m

L	m
M	l
L	m
M	l

Who Am I?

Directions: Listen to an adult read the poem. Then, talk about the questions.

I fly in the yard on
a bright summer day.

The people outside
stay out of my way.

They are yelling and running
and waving their arms.

I wish that they knew
I mean no harm.

If only they looked
closely at me.

They would know I'm just a
sweet-as-honey bumblebee.

1. Who is the character in the poem?
2. Where does the poem take place?
3. Why do you think people in the poem yell and run away from the bee?

I'm Happy

Directions: Draw what makes you happy. Trace the word. Share your drawing.

happy

Talk About It! What did you draw? Why did you draw that? What details can you add?

Animal Letter

Directions: Trace the letter. Make it into an animal.

Number Message

Directions: Color the boxes.

Color Code

1 2 3 = Blue   4 5 6 = Orange

4	5	6	4	6	5	4	6
1	6	4	2	5	2	1	3
2	5	5	3	4	6	3	6
3	4	4	1	6	4	2	4
2	6	6	2	5	5	3	6
3	1	2	3	6	4	1	4
2	5	5	1	4	6	2	5
1	4	4	3	6	4	1	6
3	5	6	2	5	5	3	4
1	4	4	1	4	1	2	3
4	6	5	4	5	6	4	6

Count These

Directions: Touch and count how many. Circle the correct number.

1 

4 5 6

2 

5 6 7

3 

7 8 9

4 

6 7 8

Color the Shapes

Directions: Color the shapes to match these:

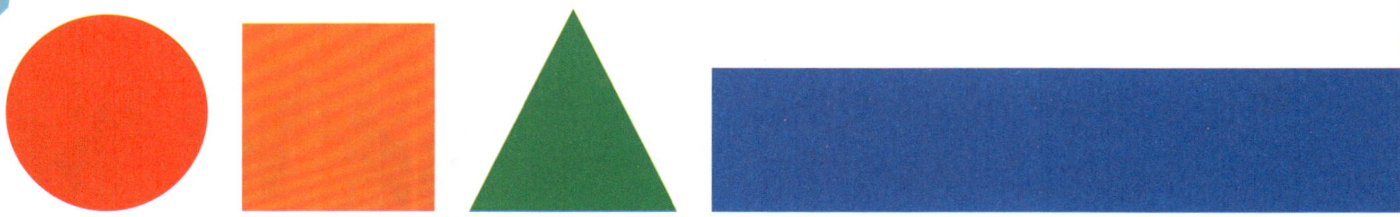

Slow and Easy Wins!

Directions: Connect the dots in order. Color the picture.

I Spy

Number of Players

2–6

Directions

1. One player looks around the room and finds an object. Then, they give a clue to the other player. The clue is to say the object's name one sound at a time. (For example, duh-eh-ss-k).
2. The other players blend the sounds together to name the word (for example, desk). The first player to say the word correctly earns 1 point.
3. Going clockwise, the next player begins the next round by choosing an object to name.
4. Continue playing until one player reaches 10 points.

Adaptations

- Say the sounds closer together so the word is more apparent to make the game easier.
- Play with only multi-syllable words to make the game more difficult.

Week 7

This week, you will practice these important skills:

- writing the letters *N* and *O*
- reading a story
- illustrating favorite activities
- drawing objects
- matching colors to numbers
- counting and writing numbers
- finding the correct shapes
- coloring pictures
- playing a racing game

Practice N and O

Directions: Trace and write the letters. Color the *Nn*'s red. Color the *Oo*'s blue.

Oo Oo

Nn Nn

n n

N o

o O N

p O

Pat the Dog

Directions: Listen to an adult read the story. Then, talk about the questions.

Pat likes to go to the park. He runs on the grass. He digs in the sand. He runs after a duck. He jumps up on a bench. Pat has fun!

1. Where does Pat go?
2. What does Pat do on the grass?
3. What does Pat run after?
4. What does Pat jump up on?

Hot Weather

Directions: Draw something you like to do when it is hot. Trace the word. Share your drawing.

hot

Talk About It!

What did you draw? Why did you draw that? What details can you add?

Flower Drawing

Directions: Draw the other half of the flower.

Beach Number Match

Directions: Color the picture.

Color Code

1 = red
2 = blue
3 = light blue
4 = yellow
5 = brown
6 = black
7 = pink

Counting Challenge

Directions: Touch and count the blocks. Write the number.

1

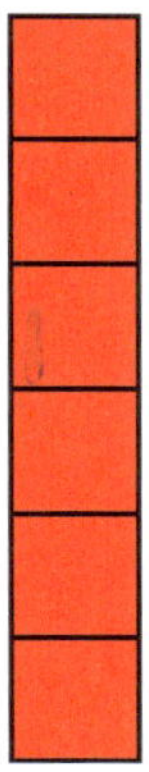

2

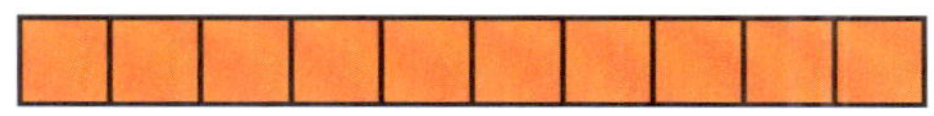

3

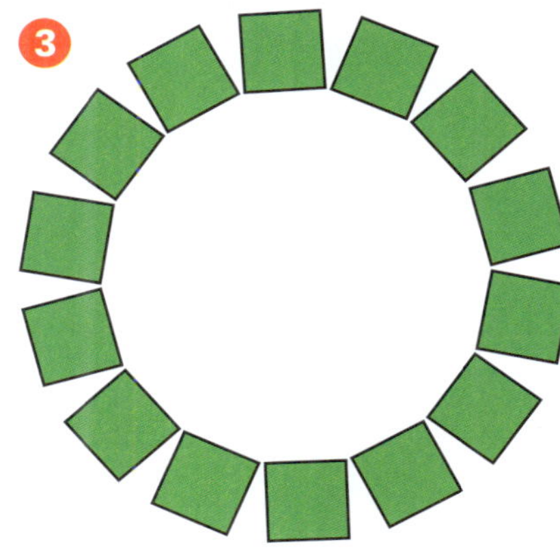

Make a triangle of 12 objects.

Find the Shapes

Directions: Mark the shapes.

1. Circle the triangles.

2. Circle the squares.

3. Underline the circles.

4. Underline the rectangles.

Color Work

Directions: Color yellow items yellow. Color pink items pink. Color red items red.

Short Racers

Number of Players

2

Materials

- *Race Numbers* (page 115)
- *Race Game Boards* (page 117)
- 2 types of small objects (for example, buttons or paper clips)

Directions

1. Cut apart the *Race Numbers* on page 115. Shuffle them and place them facedown in a pile.
2. Cut apart the *Race Game Boards* on page 117. Give one to each player.
3. The youngest player goes first. They turn over a card and move the counter to the matching number on either of the racetracks on their game board. **Note:** Counters may only move one space at a time, so if the number is not one of the next numbers on the track, the counter remains still.
4. Players take turns following the same procedure until one player reaches the finish line.

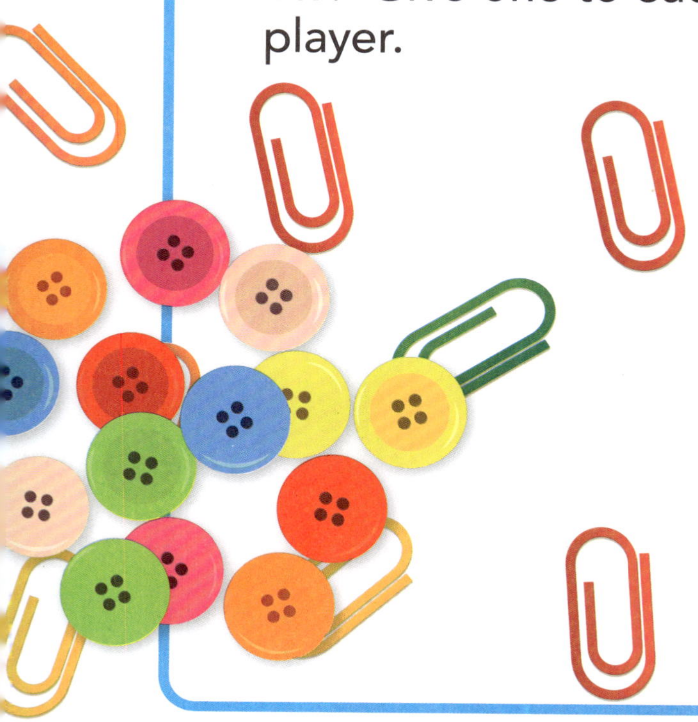

Week 8

This week, you will practice these important skills:

- writing the letters *P* and *R*
- reading a story
- illustrating where you live
- creating numbers with dough
- counting groups
- counting and matching groups
- drawing shape pictures
- coloring categories
- playing an ABC search game

Practice P and R

Directions: Trace and write the letters. Match the letters.

P p P p

R r R r

P r

R p

R p

P r

Tim's New Pet

Directions: Listen to an adult read the story. Then, answer the questions.

Tim has a new pet. He did not get it at a pet shop. The pet came to Tim's house. The pet made a brown home near Tim's window. The pet is blue. Guess what it is!

1. Tim did not get his pet at a pet shop. Why not?
   - Ⓐ His mom gave it to him.
   - Ⓑ It came to Tim's house.
   - Ⓒ It came in the window.

2. Where did it make its home?
   - Ⓐ in Tim's room
   - Ⓑ in Tim's box
   - Ⓒ near Tim's window

Home Sweet Home

Directions: Draw your home. Trace the word. Share your drawing.

home

Talk About It!

What details can you add to your picture?

Dough Number

Materials

- pencil
- white paper
- molding dough or clay

Directions

1. Trace the numbers.
2. Choose a number. Write it big on a sheet of paper.
3. Roll the dough between your hands or on a table or tray to form long, skinny rolls. Place the rolls on the lines of the number to form the number in dough.
4. You may wish to repeat these steps for different numbers.

0 1

2 3

4 5

6 7

8 9

Number Data

Directions: Touch and count the dots. Color the objects.

Color Code

1 = red	3 = green	5 = orange
2 = blue	4 = yellow	6 = purple

Count and Match

Directions: Touch and count the objects. Draw a line to match the number.

1

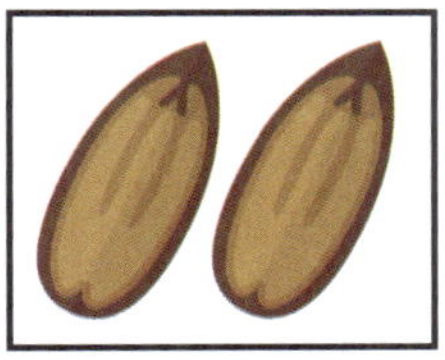

2

3

Build with Shapes

Directions: Follow the steps.

1. Outline the star in yellow.
2. Outline the triangles in green.
3. Outline the rectangles in black.
4. Outline the circle in red.

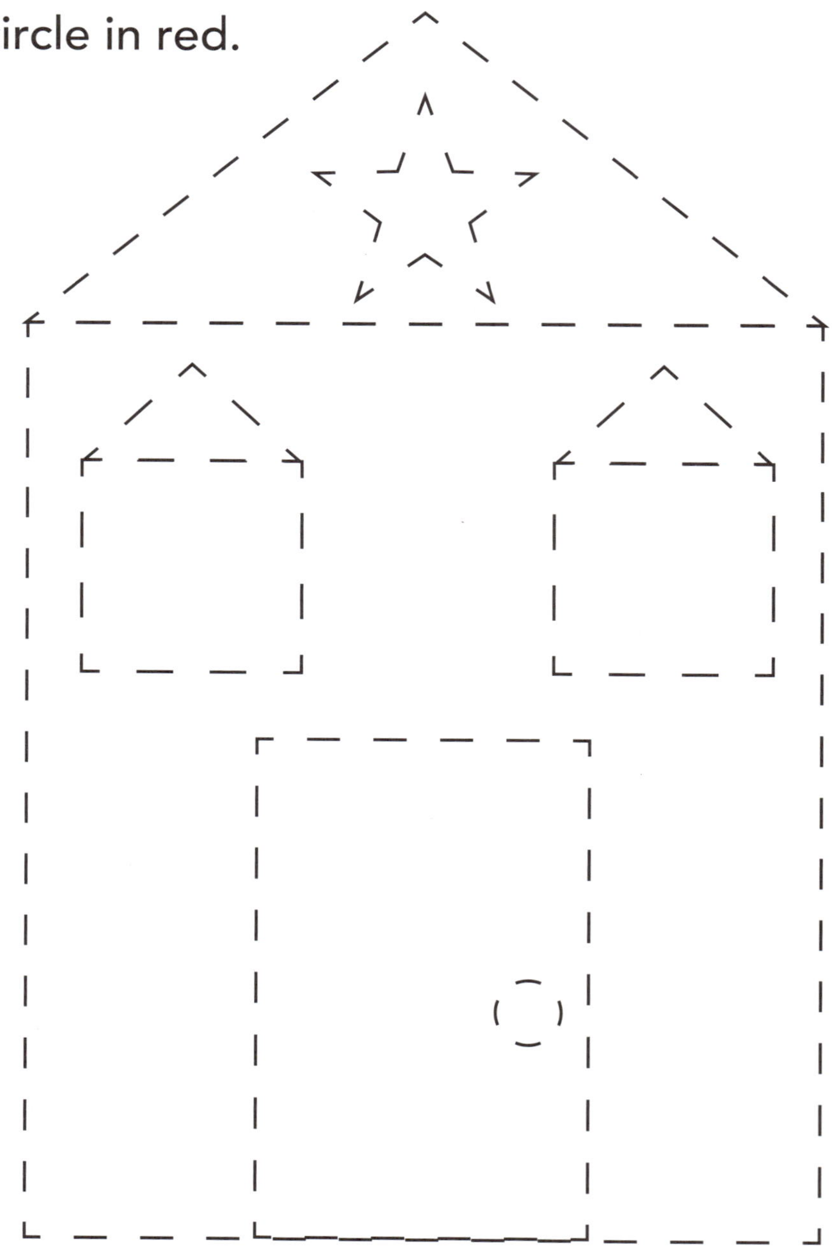

Categories

Directions: Circle the pictures that match.

animals			
foods			
toys			
numbers	3	7	K

Alphabet Scavenger Hunt

Number of Players

2–6

Directions

1. Work as a team to find an object in the house that begins with each letter of the alphabet beginning with the letter *a*. **Note:** If you are playing with an adult, you may wish to look outside, too.
2. Once you have found an object, say the letter's name and what it stands for (for example, say, "*A* is for apple.")
3. Continue finding objects for each letter in the alphabet. You may wish to draw each object you find.

Adaptations

- Play the game with fewer letters to make the game easier. For example, you may choose to find the first 10 letters of the alphabet.
- Find more than one object that begins with each letter to make the game more difficult.

Week 9

This week, you will practice these important skills:

- writing the letters *S* and *T*
- reading a nonfiction text
- illustrating things that make you laugh
- making handprint art
- playing a counting game
- counting objects
- finding shapes
- counting objects and writing numbers
- playing a letter sounds game

Practice S and T

Directions: Trace and write the letters. Color the *Ss*'s red. Color the *Tt*'s blue.

S s S s

T t T t

T S

t s

s S u

T t

Move It

Directions: Listen to an adult read the story. Then, answer the questions.

You can take very good care of your body. One good way is to move it! Play a sport. Run and go. Groove to a song. Move your body! Your body will love you for it.

1. Which is a way to dance?
   - Ⓐ groove
   - Ⓑ run
   - Ⓒ play

2. What do you groove to?
   - Ⓐ a sport
   - Ⓑ a song
   - Ⓒ a book

LOL

Directions: Draw something funny. Trace the word. Share your drawing.

funny

Talk About It! What did you draw? Why did you draw that? What details can you add?

Handprint Art

Materials

- white paper
- paint
- paintbrush
- crayons

Directions

1. Have an adult paint your hand. Press your hand down on a sheet of paper to make a handprint.
2. Allow the paint to dry. Use crayons to add details to your handprint to make it into an animal or another object.
3. Share your handprint art with a friend. Describe the details you added to your handprint.

Number Tic-Tac-Toe

Directions: Play tic-tac-toe with a friend. Use different colors to mark your boxes with *X*'s and *O*'s. Count up to each number before you mark it.

4	6	9
5	3	1
2	7	8

7	2	1
9	5	3
4	8	6

9	1	4
2	6	8
3	7	5

8	5	3
4	9	2
1	6	7

Count the Balls and Bats!

Directions: Touch and count the balls and bats. Then, follow the steps.

1. 

How many balls?

Circle the bats that show the same.

2. 

How many balls?

Circle the bats that show the same.

Find the Answer

Directions: Fill in the correct letter.

1. Which shape is a triangle?

Ⓐ 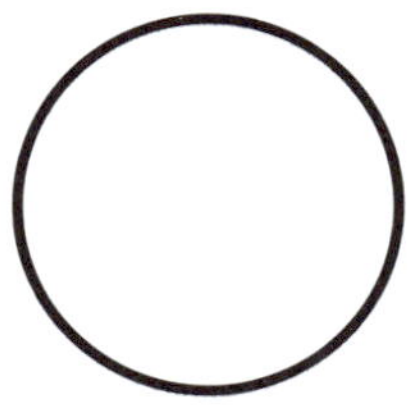

Ⓑ 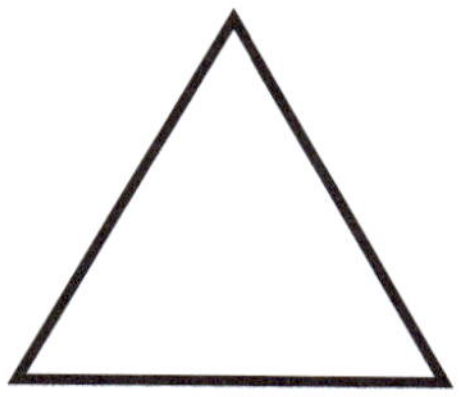

Ⓒ 

Ⓓ 

2. Which shape is a square?

Ⓐ 

Ⓑ 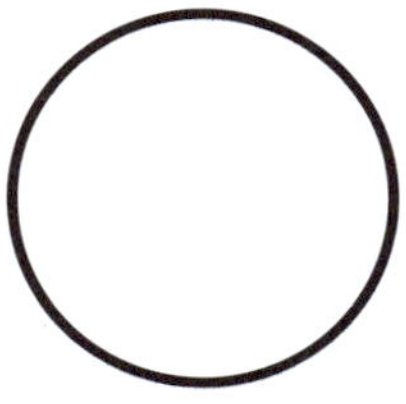

Ⓒ 

Ⓓ 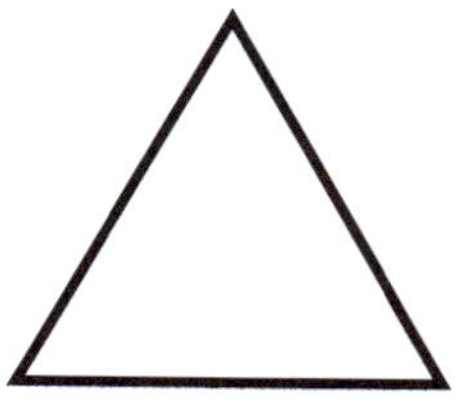

Making Butterflies

Directions: Match the dots on the right wings. Write the total number of dots.

1 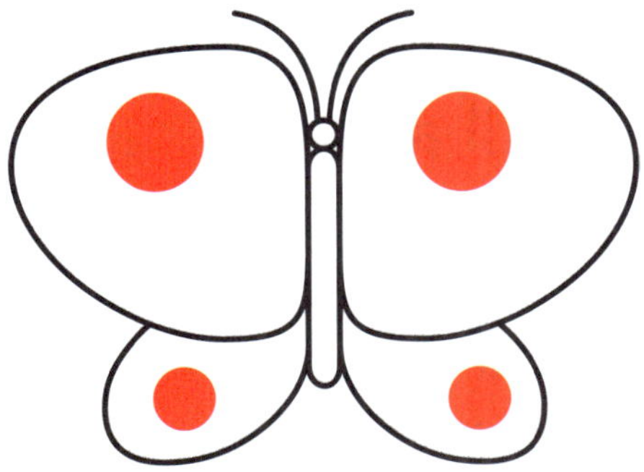

4

2 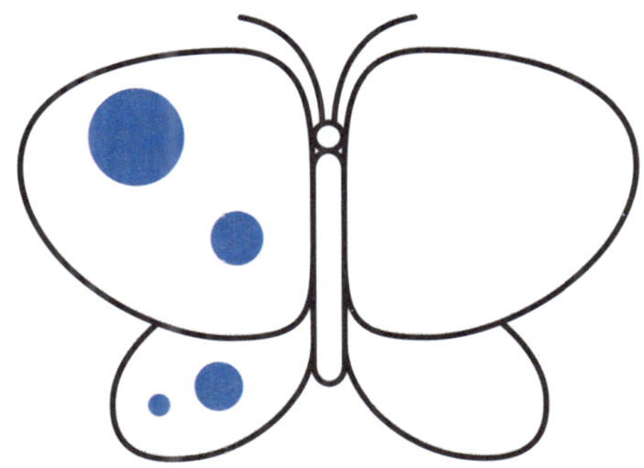

3 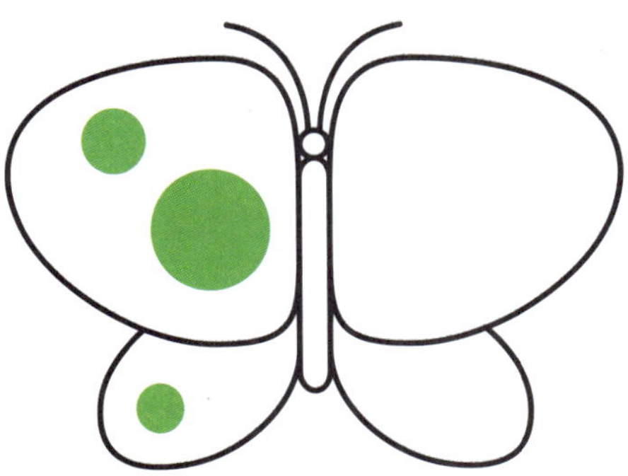

4 

I'm Going on a Trip

Number of Players

2–6

Directions

1. Choose a letter to begin the game. Review the sound the letter makes.

2. One player begins by saying, "I'm going on a trip, and I'm bringing a _____." The player names a word that begins with the letter chosen for this round of the game (for example, "I'm going on a trip, and I'm bringing a ball").

3. The next player repeats the first player's sentence, and adds a new word that begins with the same letter (for example, "I'm going on a trip, and I'm bringing a ball and balloons.").

4. Continue playing until a player cannot remember all the words that have been said or cannot think of a new word.

Adaptations

- Think of many words beginning with the chosen sound before playing the game to make the game easier. Draw quick pictures of the words if needed.
- To make it more challenging, begin with the letter A and have each player think of a word that begins with the next letter of the alphabet.

Picture Cards Set 1

Directions: Use these cards with the *Go Rhyme* activity on page 22.

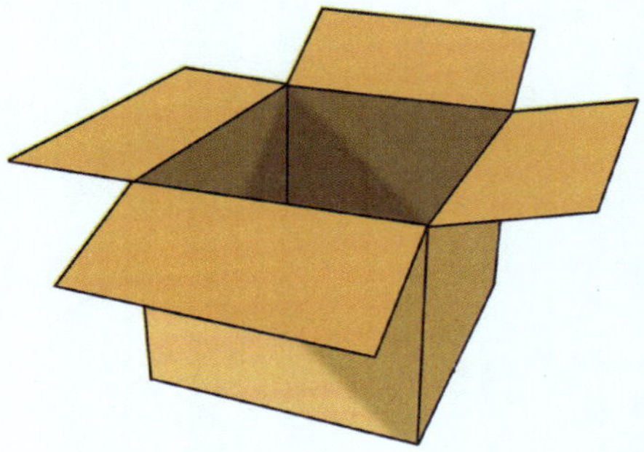

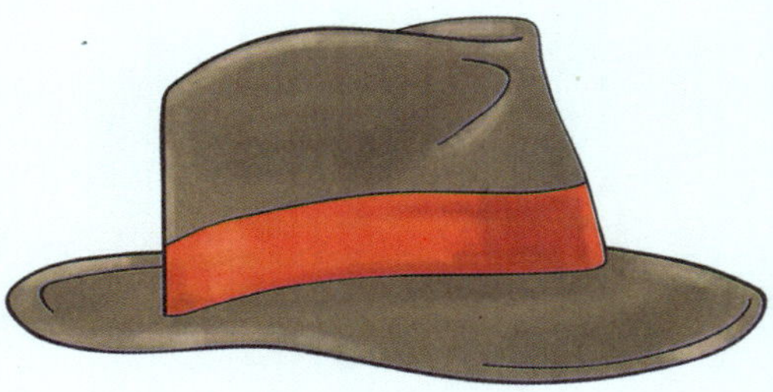

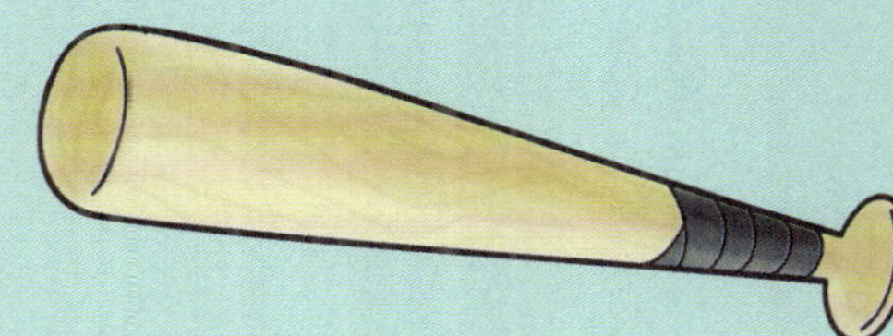

Go Rhyme	Go Rhyme
Go Rhyme	Go Rhyme
Go Rhyme	Go Rhyme
Go Rhyme	Go Rhyme

Picture Cards Set 2

Directions: Use these cards with the *Go Rhyme* activity on page 22.

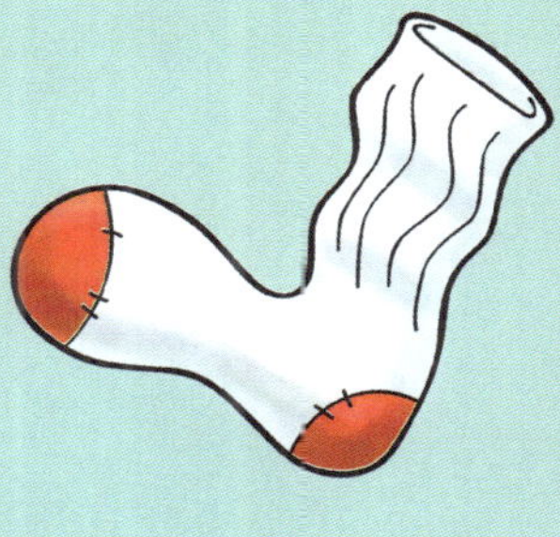

Go Rhyme	Go Rhyme
Go Rhyme	Go Rhyme
Go Rhyme	Go Rhyme
Go Rhyme	Go Rhyme

Number Cards

Directions: Use these cards with the *Action Numbers* activity on page 32, *The Number Game* activity on page 52, and the *Fill Your Basket* activity on page 62.

0	1	2
3	4	5
6	7	8
9		

Action Numbers
The Number Game
Fill Your Basket

Action Numbers
The Number Game
Fill Your Basket

Action Numbers
The Number Game
Fill Your Basket

Action Numbers
The Number Game
Fill Your Basket

Action Numbers
The Number Game
Fill Your Basket

Action Numbers
The Number Game
Fill Your Basket

Action Numbers
The Number Game
Fill Your Basket

Action Numbers
The Number Game
Fill Your Basket

Action Numbers
The Number Game
Fill Your Basket

Action Numbers
The Number Game
Fill Your Basket

Uppercase Letter Cards

Directions: Use these cards with the *The Gathering Game* activity on page 42.

A	B	C	D	E
F	G	H	I	J
K	L	M	N	O
P	Q	R	S	T
U	V	W	X	Y
Z				

The Gathering Game	The Gathering Game	The Gathering Game	The Gathering Game	The Gathering Game
The Gathering Game	The Gathering Game	The Gathering Game	The Gathering Game	The Gathering Game
The Gathering Game	The Gathering Game	The Gathering Game	The Gathering Game	The Gathering Game
The Gathering Game	The Gathering Game	The Gathering Game	The Gathering Game	The Gathering Game
The Gathering Game	The Gathering Game	The Gathering Game	The Gathering Game	The Gathering Game
				The Gathering Game

Calculator Cards

Directions: Use these cards with the *The Number Game* activity on page 52.

Player 2

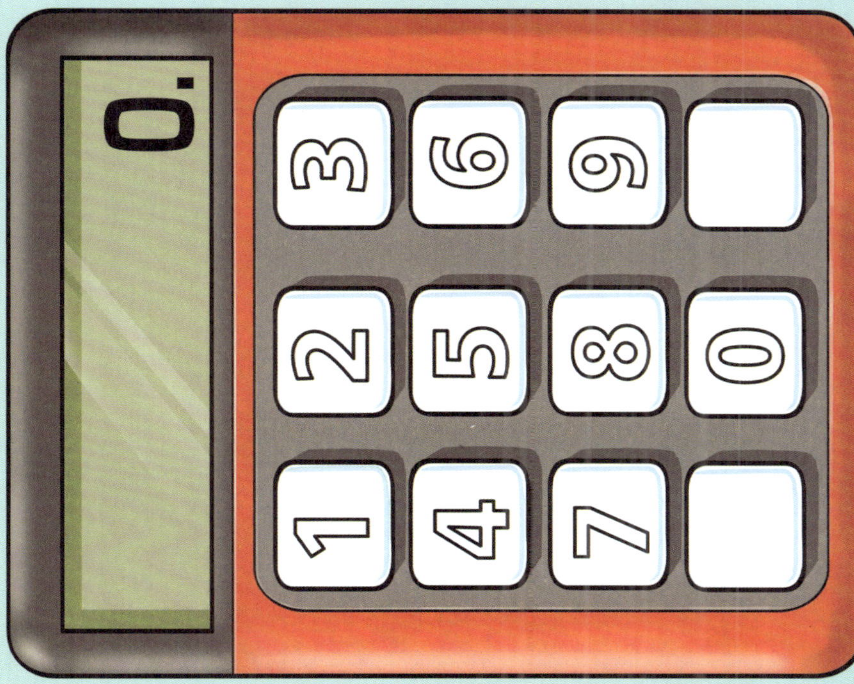

Player 1

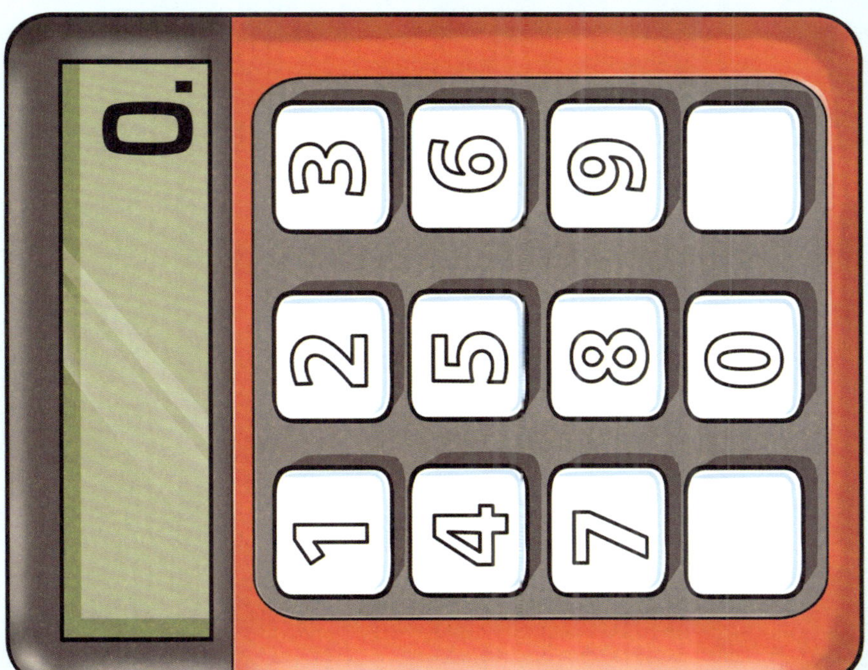

The Number Game

The Number Game

Basket Cards

Directions: Use these cards with the *Fill Your Basket* activity on page 62.

Player 2

Player 1

Fill Your Basket

Fill Your Basket

Race Numbers

Directions: Use these cards with the *Short Racers* activity on page 82.

1	1	1	2
2	2	3	3
3	4	4	4
5	5	5	6
6	6		

Short Racers	Short Racers	Short Racers	Short Racers
Short Racers	Short Racers	Short Racers	Short Racers
Short Racers	Short Racers	Short Racers	Short Racers
Short Racers	Short Racers	Short Racers	Short Racers
		Short Racers	Short Racers

Race Game Boards

Directions: Use these cards with the *Short Racers* activity on page 82.

Finish		Finish	
5	1	5	1
4	3	4	3
2	6	2	6
5	4	5	4
3	1	3	1
6	5	6	5
2	3	2	3
1	4	1	4
Start for Player 1		Start for Player 2	

Player 2	Player 1

Answer Key

Week 1

Practice A and B (page 14)

Check that the letters have been traced and closely resemble the model letters.

Make sure all lowercase letters have been colored in with the correct color.

X Marks the Spot (page 15)

1. the pirate and the parrot
2. the ship or on the water
3. The *X* on the map blows away.

Favorite Treat (page 16)

Check that the drawing includes a favorite treat.

Dot Art (page 17)

Check that the art includes the letter of the child's first name.

House Number Match (page 18)

Crazy Counting (page 19)

Check that response includes each voice when counting to 10.

Shapes Everywhere! (page 20)

Watch that the child points to correct shapes as directed.

Find the Pictures (page 21)

Check that the dots to make a picture of an apple have been connected and it has been colored.

Go Rhyme (page 22)

Check that players take turns saying rhyming words.

Week 2

Practice C and D (page 24)

Check that the letters have been traced and closely resemble the model letters.

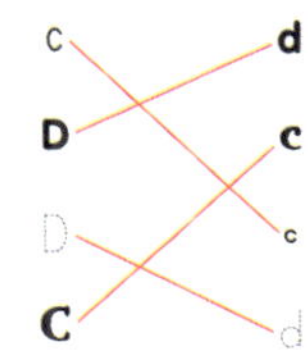

The Best Invention (page 25)

1. The child's response may include: they come in all sizes, are made for all ages, babies can ride in a trailer pulled by them, you can pedal with your hands or feet, they don't need gas, you can get exercise.
2. They don't need gas, and you can get exercise from them.
3. Check that the child's opinion states what a new bike would be able to do.

Playtime (page 26)

Check that the drawing includes something to play with.

Plant Creations (page 27)

Check that the plant parts are used in the creation.

Number Maze (page 28)

Check that the maze has been completed.

Count and Write (page 29)

1. 1
2. 2
3. 3
4. 4
5. 5

Trace the Shapes (page 30)

Check that all shapes have been traced and named.

Blue, Blue, I See You (page 31)

Check that all drawings are of something that is blue.

Answer Key

Action Numbers (page 32)

Check that the players are performing the actions the correct number of times.

Week 3

Practice E and F (page 34)

Check that the letters have been traced and closely resemble the model letters.

Make sure all lowercase letters have been colored in with the correct color.

Jack and Jill (page 35)

1. yes
2. no
3. no

Weather (page 36)

Check that the drawing includes a picture of the weather.

It's the Same (page 37)

The paint should look similar on both sides. The child's explanation of the similarity should be logical.

Zigzag Parking Lot (page 38)

Check that the child is counting from 1 to 10 while parking the car.

How Many Apples? (page 39)

1. 7
2. 6
3. 1
4. 4

Name the Shapes (page 40)

Check that the names are connected to the appropriate shapes.

Color by Shape (page 41)

The Gathering Game (page 42)

Check that the players are choosing items that begin with the correct letter.

Week 4

Practice G and H (page 44)

Check that the letters have been traced and closely resemble the model letters.

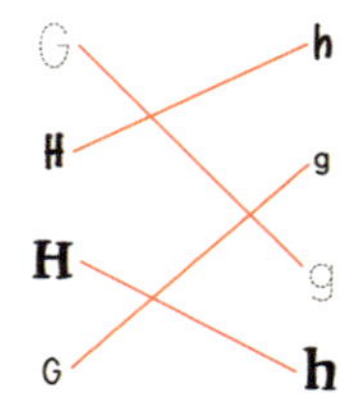

The Campout (page 45)

1. a boy and his dad
2. He was scared.
3. in a tent in the backyard

Friends (page 46)

Check that the drawing includes a picture of a friend.

Blow Art (page 37)

Check that the child is blowing the paint with a straw onto a piece of paper. Discuss what happens when the child blows lightly and harder.

Flower Number Match (page 48)

Sort and Count! (page 49)

1. 4 balls
2. 3 bats
3. 6 suns
4. 4 clouds

Answer Key

Which Shape? (page 50)

three sides: triangle

four corners: square

curved: circle

Story Time Logic (page 51)

1. Sam
2. Maya
3. Jane

The Number Game (page 52)

Check that both players have colored in all calculator buttons.

Week 5

Practice I and J (page 54)

Check that the letters have been traced and closely resemble the model letters.

Make sure all lowercase letters have been colored in with the correct color.

Good Hunters (page 55)

1. Tigers are big, wild cats.
2. Tigers can have orange, black, and white stripes.
3. Tigers hunt for monkeys, fish, and deer.

Book Time (page 56)

Check that the drawing includes a picture of a character from a book.

Hidden Shape (page 57)

Check that the shape that appears matches the object traced.

Number Search (page 58)

Check that the colors match the correct numbers.

Fill a Jar (page 59)

1. 6 dots in the jar
2. 9 dots in the jar

Make the Shapes (page 60)

Check that the drawings have followed each step.

Does Not Belong (page 61)

1. a cupcake
2. an elephant
3. a school
4. a dog

Fill Your Basket (page 62)

Check that the players are placing the correct number of counters in their baskets.

Week 6

Practice L and M (page 64)

Check that the letters have been traced and closely resemble the model letters.

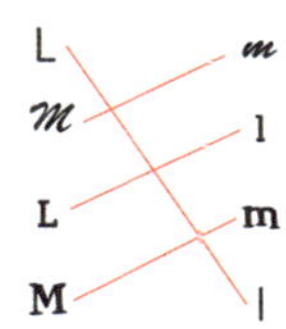

Who Am I? (page 65)

1. bee
2. the yard
3. They think the bee will sting them.

I'm Happy (page 66)

Check that the drawing includes a picture of something that makes the child happy.

Animal Letter (page 67)

Check that the letter has animal features.

Number Message (page 68)

The secret message is: HI

Count These (page 69)

1. 4 pigs
2. 6 birds
3. 9 alligators
4. 8 kittens

Color the Shapes (page 70)

Check that each shape is colored with the correct color.

Answer Key

Slow and Easy Wins! (page 71)

Check that the picture has been colored.

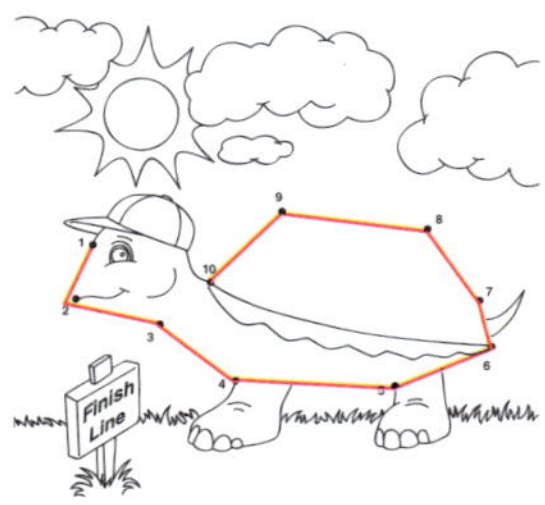

I Spy (page 72)

Check that the players are saying each sound.

Week 7

Practice N and O (page 74)

Check that the letters have been traced and closely resemble the model letters.

Make sure all lowercase letters have been colored in with the correct color.

Pat the Dog (page 75)

1. to the park
2. runs
3. a duck
4. a bench

Hot Weather (page 76)

Check that the drawing includes a picture of something the child likes to do in hot weather and the word has been traced.

Flower Drawing (page 77)

Check that the drawing resembles the other half of the flower.

Beach Number Match (page 78)

Counting Challenge (page 79)

1. 6
2. 10
3. 14

Check that 12 objects are used to create a triangle.

Find the Shapes (page 80)

1. 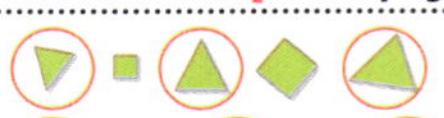
2. 
3. 
4. 

Color Work (page 81)

Yellow: cheese, banana, corn, and chick

Pink: pig and flamingo

Red: apple, stop sign

Short Racers (page 82)

Check that the players move to the correct spaces on the racetrack.

Week 8

Practice P and R (page 84)

Check that the letters have been traced and closely resemble the model letters.

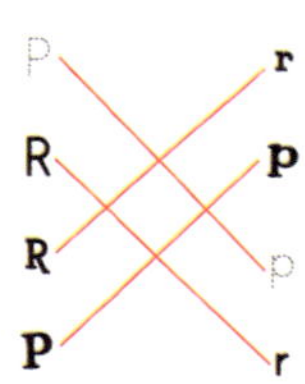

Tim's New Pet (page 85)

1. B
2. C

Home Sweet Home (page 86)

Check that the drawing includes a picture of where the child lives.

Dough Number (page 87)

Check that the dough is formed into a number.

Answer Key

Number Data (page 88)

Check that the colors match the correct number of dots.

Count and Match (page 89)

1. 2 seeds
2. 3 nuts
3. 6 fish

Build with Shapes (page 90)

Check to see that the child followed instructions.

Categories (page 91)

animals: bird and snake

foods: banana and hamburger

toys: ball and toy top

numbers: 3 and 7

Alphabet Scavenger Hunt (page 92)

Check that the players are matching the correct letters to the objects.

Week 9

Practice S and T (page 94)

Check that the letters have been traced and closely resemble the model letters.

Make sure all lowercase letters have been colored in with the correct color.

Move It (page 95)

1. A
2. B

LOL (page 96)

Check that the drawing includes a picture of something funny.

Handprint Art (page 97)

Check to see that the painting includes animal features or other details.

Number Tic-Tac-Toe (page 98)

Make sure both players name the numbers before they mark them.

Count the Balls and Bats! (page 99)

1. 3 balls; circle 3 bats
2. 4 balls; circle 4 bats

Find the Answer (page 100)

1. B
2. C

Making Butterflies (page 101)

1. 4 dots
2. 8 dots
3. 6 dots
4. 2 dots

I'm Going on a Trip (page 102)

Check that the players are saying words that start with the correct letter.

Doodles

Doodles

Doodles

Doodles

Doodles